ALVIN TRESSELT

THE DEAD TREE

Illustrated by Charles Robinson

Parents' Magazine Press

New York

With thanks, to Lilian Moore

It stood tall in the forest.
For a hundred years or more the oak tree
had grown and spread its shade.
Birds nested in its shelter.
Squirrels made their homes in ragged bundles
of sticks and leaves held high in the branches.
And in the fall they garnered their winter food
from the rich rain of acorns that fell
from the tree.

Tucked under its gnarled roots, small creatures
found safety from the fox and owl.
Slowly, slowly, over the years the forest soil
increased as the brown leathery leaves,
shaken down by the autumn winds, moldered
under the snow.

But even as the tree grew, life gnawed
at its heart. Carpenter ants tunneled through
the strength of the oak. Termites ate out
passageways in wondrous patterns.
A broken limb let the dusty spores of fungus
enter the heartwood of the tree.
And a rot spread inside the healthy bark.

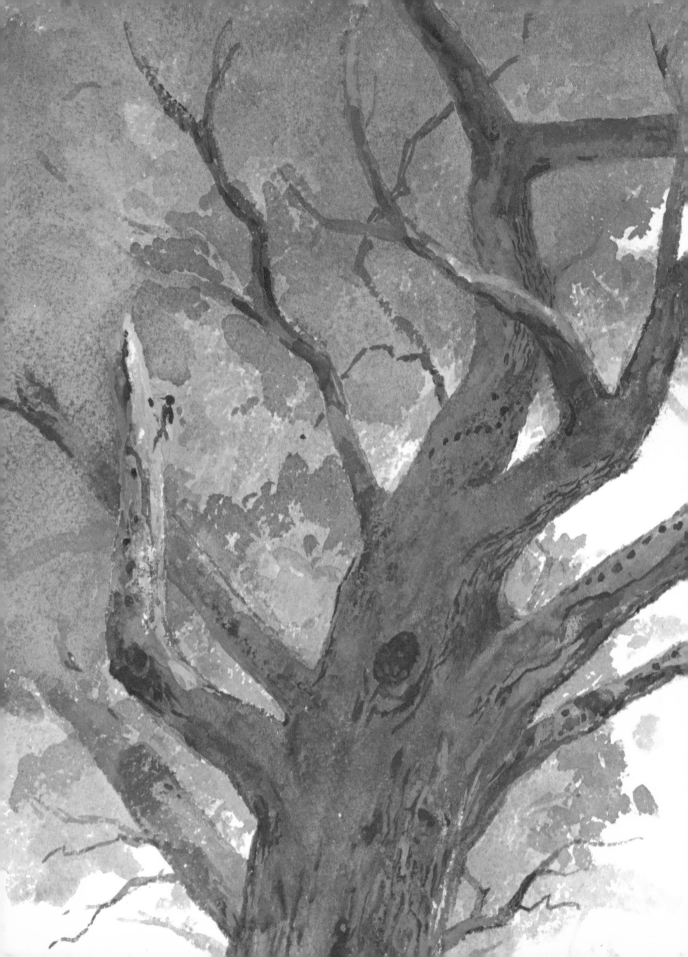

Year by year the tree grew weaker
as its enemies worked.
Each spring fewer and fewer leaves unfolded,
and its great reaching branches turned gray
with death. Woodpeckers peppered the limbs
with holes, looking for the tasty grubs and beetles
that had tunneled the wood.
And here and there they dug bigger holes
to hold their babies.

In winter storms, one by one, the great branches
broke and crashed to the floor of the forest
until there remained only the proud trunk,
holding its broken arms up to the sky.
Now it was the autumn weather, and it was
long and lazy. Yellow-gray and misty mornings,
middays filled with false summer warmth,
and the nights pierced with frost.

Then came a day of hurricane wind and slashing rain,
and as the fierce wind shrieked through the forest
the tree split off and crashed to the ground.
There it lay shattered, with only a jagged stump
to mark where it had stood for so long.

The cruel days of winter followed.
A family of deer mice settled into a hole
that had once held an arching branch.
A rabbit found protection from the biting wind
in the rotted center of the trunk.
And the ants and termites, the dormant grubs
and silent fungus waited out the winter weather,
under the bark and deep in the wood.

In the spring the young sun warmed the forest floor,
and acorns sprouted to replace the fallen giant.
Now new life took over the dead tree.

Old woodpecker holes made snug homes for chipmunks.
The hollow center of the trunk sheltered a family
of raccoons. While beneath the bark spread
the wood-eating fungus, ghost-white and sulphur yellow.
And deep inside, the carpenter ants and the termites
continued their digging and eating.

On the underside where the trunk lay half buried
in the damp and musty leaf loam the mosses stitched
a green carpet softer than the softest wool.
Fragile ferns clustered in its shadow,
mushrooms popped up out of the decaying mold,
and scarlet clumps of British soldiers
sprinkled the loosening bark.

The years passed, and the oak-hard wood grew soft and punky.
It crawled with a hundred thousand grubs and beetles.
Centipedes with their scrambling scurrying legs,
snails and slugs, all fed on the rotting wood.
And earthworms made their way through the feast, helping
to turn the tree once more into earth.

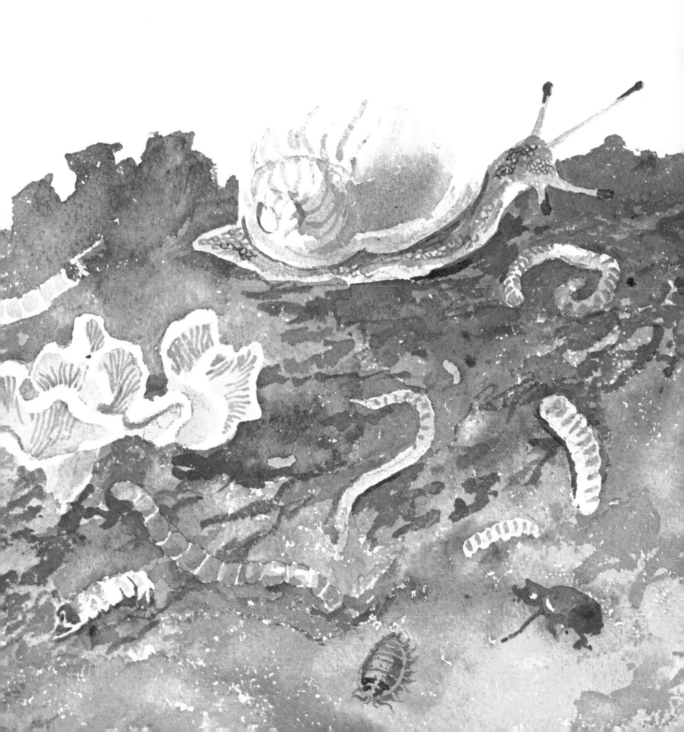

Pale shelf fungus clung to the sides like clusters of giant clamshells, eating away and growing as the tree decayed.

A skunk came waddling by with her string of babies.
Sniffing at the wood she ripped into its softness with her claws
to uncover the scrambling life inside, and eagerly
the family feasted. Secretive forest birds scratched and picked
for grubs and worms, pulling the tree apart bit by bit.
While the melting winter snows and soft spring rains
hastened the rotting of the wood.

And in this way, as new trees grew in strength
from acorns that had fallen long years ago,
the great oak returned to the earth.
On the ground there remained only a brown ghost
of richer loam where the proud tree had come to rest.

Alvin Tresselt is the distinguished author of more than twenty-five books for children, including the Caldecott Medal winner, *White Snow, Bright Snow*. He is represented on the Parents' list by *A Thousand Lights and Fireflies*, *The Legend of the Willow Plate*, *Bonnie Bess the Weathervane Horse* and *How Far is Far?* Mr. Tresselt has been chairman of the Juvenile Writers Committee of the Authors' Guild and Vice President of the Children's Book Council. He also served as editor of *Humpty Dumpty's Magazine* for thirteen years. Mr. Tresselt lives with his wife and two daughters in West Redding, Connecticut.

Charles Robinson was born in Morristown, New Jersey. He received his B.A. at Harvard and his law degree from the University of Virginia Law School. After service in the U.S. Army Signal Corps, he practiced law in New Jersey and from 1960 to 1968 was a staff attorney for the Mutual Benefit Life Insurance Company. It was in 1968 that he became a full-time artist and since then he has illustrated well over a dozen books for young readers, including *Giants Are Very Brave People*, published by Parents' Magazine Press, as well as *Yuri and the Mooneygoats*, *The Sometimes Island* and *The Good Morrow*. Mr. Robinson, with his wife and three children, lives in Morristown, New Jersey.

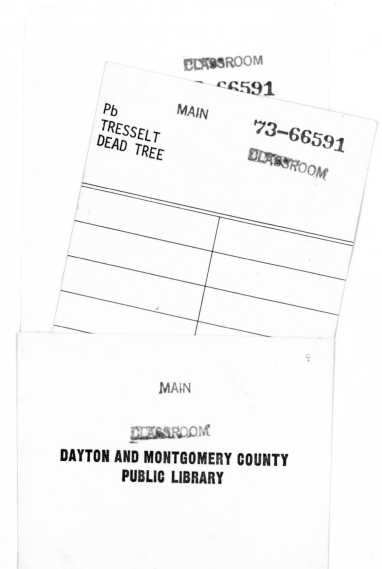